FABULOUS BIRTHDAY CAKES

Consultant Editor:
Valerie Ferguson

HERMES
HOUSE

Contents

Introduction

How can you celebrate a birthday without a special cake? Whether you are eight or eighty, there is something magical about the moment when you cut it. This book is packed with fabulous ideas for every kind of birthday cake. There are imaginative novelty cakes, elegant confections decorated with flowers and extravagant chocolate cakes. There are suggestions for "landmark" birthdays, such as a twenty-first, and a wealth of ideas for personalizing cakes. It is easy to change the decoration to match personal tastes.

Most of the cakes are based on a simple recipe, and basic icings and glazes are used throughout. Detailed step-by-step instructions guide you through the often intricate and time-consuming processes. While all the cakes look spectacular, many are surprisingly easy to make. Sugarpaste icing, for example, is so versatile that even the complete beginner can achieve really striking effects, while handling royal icing takes a little more practice. A helpful introduction offers advice on useful equipment, hints and tips for successful cake making and some basic preparation techniques.

Spending time, care and imagination on the perfect birthday cake is one of the nicest presents you can give.

Equipment

To obtain the best results when making cakes, it is necessary to have a selection of good equipment.

• Accurate weighing scales, measuring spoons and jugs are available in both metric and imperial measurements. Always measure level when using spoons unless otherwise instructed by the recipe.

• A set of mixing bowls in various sizes and a selection of wooden spoons are essential items. However, an electric hand-held beater will save time and make cake making easier.

• Cake tins: the most regularly used are round or square in sizes 15 cm/6 in, 20 cm/8 in and 25 cm/10 in.

• Cooling racks: at least two racks are useful for cake making and decorating.

• A serrated knife for cutting the cooled cake without it crumbling.

• A pastry brush for brushing cakes with apricot glaze.

• A heavy rolling pin for rolling out marzipan and sugarpaste icing.

• Pastry, small biscuit and cocktail cutters are available in various shapes and sizes and are useful for cutting sugarpaste icing shapes.

• A palette knife for spreading.

• Piping bags and a variety of nozzles (or you can use greaseproof paper cones with the nozzles).

• A turntable is not essential but makes icing much easier.

• Sable paintbrushes for painting fine details on to cakes.

• Silver cake boards for presenting decorated cakes.

Above: A selection of useful items for cake making and decorating.

Successful Cake Making

Following the simple guidelines below will help to ensure your cake making is as successful and trouble-free as possible.

• Always use the correct shape and size of tin for the recipe and make sure the tin is properly prepared and lined.

• Check that you have all the necessary ingredients to hand, that they have been measured correctly and are at the right temperature before you start mixing them together.

• Ensure soft margarine is kept chilled in the fridge to maintain the right consistency. Leave butter out to reach room temperature.

• Sift all dry ingredients to help aerate the mixture and disperse lumps.

• Use the correct sugar. Caster sugar creams more easily with fats than granulated sugar, and is used where a fine and soft texture is required. Soft brown sugar is used for some recipes when making heavier cakes.

• Use good quality fruit and peel for fruit cake recipes. Sometimes stored sultanas can become hard.

• When making cakes by hand, beat well with a wooden spoon until the mixture is light and glossy; scrape down the mixture from the sides of the bowl during beating with a plastic mixing spatula to ensure even mixing.

• If a cake is being made in a food processor or an electric mixer, be very careful not to overprocess or overbeat. Scrape down the batter with a plastic spatula during mixing.

• If ingredients have to be folded into a mixture, use a plastic spatula with a flexible blade.

• Level cake mixtures before baking.

• Check that your oven is preheated to the temperature stated in the recipe. Failure to do so will affect the rising of the cake and the cooking time.

• If the cake appears to be cooked before the given time, it may indicate that the oven is too hot; conversely, if it takes longer to cook, it means the oven is too cool.

• The temperature of the cake mixture can cause the cooking time to vary. If conditions are cold, the mixture will be cold and take longer to cook and if it is warm the cooking time will be slightly quicker.

• The surface of the cake should be evenly browned and level; if the cake is overcooked or risen to one side, then the heat in the oven is uneven or the oven shelf is not level.

Techniques

Preparing Cake Tins

Instructions vary for preparing cake tins, depending on the mixture and the baking time. Proper preparation aids turning out.

1 To grease a tin: if using butter or margarine, hold a small piece of kitchen paper (or use your fingers), to rub it all over the base and sides of the tin to make a thin, even coating. If using oil, brush a small amount on with a pastry brush.

2 To flour a tin: put a small scoop of flour in the centre of the greased tin. Tip and rotate the tin to coat the base and side. Shake out excess flour, tapping to dislodge any pockets. This will prevent the cake sticking.

Lining a Shallow Cake Tin

Lining tins is sometimes necessary to ensure that the cake comes out of the tin without breaking or sticking to the base.

1 To line the base of a tin: place the tin on a piece of greaseproof paper or baking parchment, draw around the base with a pencil and cut out the paper inside this line to fit tightly.

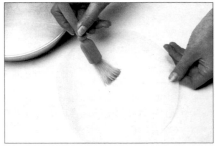

2 Grease the base and side of the tin with butter or soft margarine. If you are lining the base only, grease the paper and then place it grease-side up in the tin, which is now ready for filling. If you are lining the side as well, prepare the paper for that before greasing and inserting the base lining.

3 To line the side of a tin: cut a strip of paper long enough to wrap around the outside of the tin and overlap by 4 cm/1½ in. It should be wider than the depth by 2.5 cm/1 in.

4 Fold the strip lengthways at the 2.5 cm/1 in point and crease. Snip at regular intervals from the edge to the crease along the fold. Line the side of the tin, with the snipped part of the strip on and overlapping the base. Press the bottom lining in (Steps 1 and 2). Grease the lining paper.

5 For square and rectangular cake tins, fold the paper and crease it with your fingernail to fit snugly into the corners of the tin. Then press the bottom paper lining into place.

Lining a Deep Cake Tin

1 Place the tin on a double thickness of greaseproof paper or baking parchment. Draw around the base with a pencil. Cut out the marked shape with a pair of scissors.

2 Cut a strip of double-thickness greaseproof paper or baking parchment long enough to wrap around the outside of the tin, leaving a small overlap. It should stand 2.5 cm/1 in above the top of the tin.

3 Brush the base and side of the tin with butter or soft margarine. Place the double strip of paper inside the tin, pressing well against the side and making sharp creases if it needs to fit into corners. Place the cut-out shape in the base of the tin and press it flat.

4 Brush the base and side papers well with butter or soft margarine. Place a strip of double-thickness brown paper around the outside of the tin and tie securely with a string.

Line a baking sheet with three or four layers of brown paper and stand the tin on top.

Quick-mix Sponge Cake

Choose chocolate, lemon or orange flavouring for this light and versatile sponge cake, or leave it plain. Bake in a ring mould if you prefer.

Makes 1 x 20 cm/8 in round or 18 cm/7 in square cake

INGREDIENTS
115 g/4 oz/1 cup self-raising flour
5 ml/1 tsp baking powder
115 g/4 oz/½ cup soft margarine
115 g/4 oz/generous ½ cup caster sugar
2 eggs

FOR THE FLAVOURINGS
Chocolate: 15 ml/1 tbsp cocoa powder
 blended with 15 ml/1 tbsp boiling water
Lemon: 10 ml/2 tsp grated lemon rind
Orange: 15 ml/1 tbsp grated orange rind

1 Preheat the oven to 160°C/325°F/ Gas 3. Grease and line a 20 cm/8 in round tin or 18 cm/7 in square tin.

2 Sift together the flour and baking powder into a bowl. Add the margarine, sugar and eggs with the chosen flavourings, if using.

3 Beat with a wooden spoon for 2–3 minutes. The mixture should be pale in colour and slightly glossy.

4 Spoon the mixture into the cake tin and smooth the surface. Bake in the centre of the preheated oven for 30–40 minutes, or until a metal skewer inserted into the centre of the cake comes out clean. If you use a ring mould it will need only 25-30 minutes to cook. Turn out on to a wire rack, remove the lining paper and leave to cool completely.

Madeira Cake

This is a richer basic cake which is ideal for decorating with marzipan and royal icing or any other icing.

Makes 1 x 20 cm/8 in round or 18 cm/7 in square cake

INGREDIENTS
225 g/8 oz/2 cups plain flour
5 ml/1 tsp baking powder
225 g/8 oz/1 cup butter or margarine,
    at room temperature
225 g/8 oz/generous 1 cup caster sugar
grated rind of 1 lemon
5 ml/1 tsp vanilla essence
4 eggs

1 Preheat the oven to 160°C/325°F/ Gas 3. Grease and line a cake tin.

2 Sift together the flour and baking powder into a bowl. Set aside.

3 Cream the butter or margarine, adding the caster sugar about 30 ml/ 2 tbsp at a time, until light and fluffy. Stir in the lemon rind and vanilla essence. Add the eggs, one at a time, beating the mixture for 1 minute after each addition. Add the flour mixture and stir until just combined.

4 Pour the cake mixture into the prepared tin and tap lightly to level. Bake for about 1¼ hours, or until a metal skewer inserted into the centre comes out clean.

5 Cool in the tin on a wire rack for 10 minutes, then turn the cake out and leave to cool completely.

Light Fruit Cake

Although less rich than traditional fruit cakes, this version is still perfect for decorating with marzipan and sugarpaste or royal icing.

Makes 1 x 20 cm/8 in round or
18 cm/7 in square cake

INGREDIENTS
225 g/8 oz/1 cup butter or
    soft margarine
225 g/8 oz/generous 1 cup
    caster sugar
grated rind of 1 orange
5 eggs
300 g/11 oz/2⅔ cups plain flour
2.5 ml/½ tsp baking powder
10 ml/2 tsp ground mixed spice
175 g/6 oz/1 cup currants
175 g/6 oz/1 cup raisins
50 g/2 oz/¼ cup dried
    apricots, chopped
115 g/4 oz/¾ cup mixed peel

1 Preheat the oven to 150°C/300°F/ Gas 2. Grease a deep 20 cm/8 in round or 18 cm/7 in square tin, and line fully with a double thickness of greaseproof paper. Grease the paper.

2 Place all the ingredients in a large bowl. Stir to combine, then beat with a wooden spoon for 3–4 minutes. Spoon the mixture into the prepared tin and smooth the surface with the back of a wet metal spoon. Make a slight depression in the centre.

3 Bake in the centre of the oven for 2¾–3¼ hours, or until a metal skewer inserted into the centre comes out clean and it feels firm. Cool completely in the tin, then turn out, leaving the paper in place.

Truffle Cake Mix

This is a no-cook recipe, using leftover pieces of sponge cake.

Makes 450 g/1 lb

INGREDIENTS
175 g/6 oz plain sponge
   cake pieces
175 g/6 oz/2 cups ground almonds
75 g/3 oz/scant ⅓ cup dark brown
   muscovado sugar
5 ml/1 tsp ground
   mixed spice
pinch of ground cinnamon
finely grated rind of 1 orange
45 ml/3 tbsp freshly squeezed
   orange juice
75 ml/5 tbsp clear honey

1 Place the sponge cake pieces into the bowl of a food processor or blender and process for a few seconds to form fine crumbs.

2 Place the cake crumbs, ground almonds, sugar, spices, orange rind, orange juice and honey in a large mixing bowl. Stir well to combine into a thick, smooth mixture.

3 Use the mixture as directed in the recipe. The truffle mixture can be made and moulded into any simple shape, such as a log, sausage or balls. The moulded mixture can be covered with marzipan or sugarpaste icing.

Apricot Glaze

Use the glaze to brush cakes before applying marzipan, or use for glazing fruits on gâteaux and cakes.

Makes 450 g/1 lb/1½ cups

INGREDIENTS
450 g/1 lb/1½ cups apricot jam
45 ml/3 tbsp water

1 Place the apricot jam and water in a saucepan. Heat the mixture gently, stirring occasionally, until the jam has melted. Boil rapidly for 1 minute.

2 Remove the pan from the heat and rub the glaze through a fine-meshed sieve, pressing the fruit against the sides of the sieve with the back of a wooden spoon. Discard the apricot skins left behind in the sieve.

3 While the glaze is still warm, use a pastry brush to spread it over the entire surface of the cake.

Butter Icing

The creamy rich flavour of butter icing is popular with everyone.

Makes 350 g/12 oz/1½ cups

INGREDIENTS
225 g/8 oz/2 cups icing sugar, sifted
75 g/3 oz/6 tbsp soft margarine or
    softened butter
5 ml/1 tsp vanilla essence
10–15 ml/2–3 tsp milk

1 Put the icing sugar, margarine or butter, vanilla essence and 5 ml/1 tsp of the milk into a bowl.

2 Beat with a wooden spoon or an electric mixer until creamy. Add sufficient extra milk, a little at a time, until the icing has a light, smooth and fluffy consistency.

3 To make flavoured butter icing, follow the instructions for chocolate, coffee or citrus flavourings given below for the flavour of your choice.

FOR THE FLAVOURINGS
Chocolate: blend 15 ml/1 tbsp cocoa powder
    with 15 ml/1 tbsp hot water. Cool before
    beating into the icing.
Coffee: blend 10 ml/2 tsp coffee powder
    with 15 ml/1 tbsp hot water. Omit the milk.
    Cool, then beat the mixture into the icing.
Lemon, orange or lime: replace the vanilla
    essence and milk with lemon, orange or
    lime juice and 10 ml/2 tsp finely grated
    citrus rind. Omit the rind if using the icing
    for piping. Lightly tint the icing with food
    colouring, if wished.

Marzipan

Use marzipan on its own, under an icing or for modelling.

Makes 450 g/1 lb/3 cups

INGREDIENTS
225 g/8 oz/2 cups ground almonds
115 g/4 oz/generous ½ cup caster sugar
115 g/4 oz/1 cup icing sugar, sifted
5 ml/1 tsp lemon juice
a few drops of almond essence
1 small egg, or 1 medium egg white
food colouring (optional)

1 Stir the ground almonds and caster and icing sugars together in a bowl until evenly mixed. Make a well in the centre and add the lemon juice, almond essence and enough egg or egg white to mix to a soft, but firm dough, using a wooden spoon.

2 Form the marzipan into a ball. Lightly dust a surface with icing sugar and knead the marzipan until smooth. Wrap in clear film or store in a bag until needed. Tint by kneading in food colouring if required.

Sugarpaste Icing

This pliable icing can be coloured, moulded and shaped.

Makes 350 g/12 oz/2¼ cups

INGREDIENTS
1 egg white
15 ml/1 tbsp liquid glucose, warmed
350 g/12 oz/3 cups icing sugar, sifted

1 Put the egg white and glucose in a mixing bowl. Stir them together to break up the egg white. Add the icing sugar and mix together with a palette knife, using a chopping action, until well blended and the icing begins to bind together. Knead the mixture with your fingers until it forms a ball.

2 Knead the sugarpaste on a work surface lightly dusted with icing sugar for several minutes until smooth, soft and pliable without any cracks. If the icing is too soft, knead in some more sifted icing sugar until it reaches the right consistency.

Royal Icing

This recipe makes enough icing to cover an 18 cm/7 in cake.

Makes 675 g/1½ lb/4½ cups

INGREDIENTS
3 egg whites
about 675 g/1½ lb/6 cups icing sugar, sifted
7.5 ml/1½ tsp glycerine
a few drops of lemon juice
food colouring (optional)

1 Put the egg whites in a bowl and stir lightly with a wooden spoon to break them up. Gradually add the icing sugar, beating well with the spoon after each addition. Add enough icing sugar to make a smooth, shiny icing that has the consistency of very stiff meringue. Do not use an electric mixer as this will make the icing too fluffy.

2 Beat in the glycerine, lemon juice and food colouring, if using. Leave for 1 hour, or up to 24 hours before using, covered with damp clear film, then stir to burst any air bubbles.

Fudge Frosting

This rich, darkly delicious frosting can transform a simple sponge cake.

Makes 350 g/12 oz/2¼ cups

INGREDIENTS
50 g/2 oz/2 squares plain chocolate
225 g/8 oz/1½ cups icing sugar, sifted
50 g/2 oz/4 tbsp butter or margarine
45 ml/3 tbsp milk or single cream
5 ml/1 tsp vanilla essence

1 Break or chop the chocolate into small pieces. Put the chocolate, icing sugar, butter or margarine, milk or cream and vanilla essence in a heavy-based saucepan. Stir over a very low heat until the chocolate and butter or margarine melt. Remove from the heat and stir until evenly blended.

2 Beat the icing frequently as it cools until it thickens sufficiently to use for spreading or piping. Use immediately and work quickly once it has reached the right consistency, otherwise it will be difficult to spread.

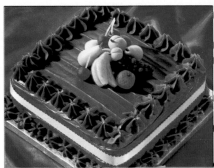

Glacé Icing

This icing can be made in just a few minutes and can be varied by adding a little food colouring or a flavouring such as coffee.

Makes 225 g/8 oz/1 cup

INGREDIENTS
225 g/8 oz/2 cups icing sugar
30–45 ml/2–3 tbsp warm water or
    fruit juice
food colouring or flavouring
    (optional)

1 Sift the icing sugar into a bowl. Using a wooden spoon, gradually stir in enough liquid to make an icing that is the consistency of thick cream. Beat until the icing is smooth. It should be thick enough to coat the back of the spoon. If it is too runny, beat in a little more sifted icing sugar.

2 Beat in a few drops of food colouring or flavouring, if using. Use immediately for coating or piping.

Sugar-frosted Flowers

These pretty, edible flowers make dainty and elegant decorations.

To cover about 20 flowers

INGREDIENTS
edible flowers, such as pansies, primroses,
    violets, roses, freesias or nasturtiums
1 egg white
caster sugar

1 Trim the stems from the flowers, leaving approximately 2 cm/¾ in if possible. Wash the flowers and dry gently on kitchen paper. Lightly beat the egg white in a small bowl and sprinkle some caster sugar on to a plate for coating the flowers.

2 Using a paintbrush, brush both sides of the petals with egg white. Hold by the stem over the plate and coat with sugar. Shake off any excess. Dry in a warm place on a board or wire rack covered with kitchen paper.

Dinosaur Cake

For a dino-crazy kid, this cake is just the ticket. Put it on a cake board or build a little scene around it.

Serves 8–10

INGREDIENTS
1 quantity Quick-mix Sponge Cake mix*
½ quantity Butter Icing*
1 quantity Truffle Cake mix*
2⅔ x quantity Sugarpaste Icing*
pink, orange, green and black food colouring
60 ml/4 tbsp Apricot Glaze*
* See Basic Cakes, Icings & Glazes

1 Preheat the oven to 180°C/350°F/ Gas 4. Grease and base line a 900 g/ 2 lb heart-shaped cake tin. Spoon in the sponge cake mixture, smooth the surface and bake for 35–40 minutes, or until a metal skewer inserted into the centre comes out clean. Turn out on to a wire rack and leave to cool.

2 Cut the cake in half vertically, then sandwich together with the butter icing to form a half heart shape. Place the cake in the centre of a 5 x 25 cm/ 2 x 10 in strip of card on its straight side. Stand on a small block of wood.

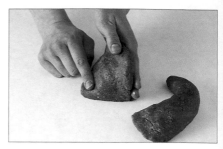

3 Divide the truffle cake mixture in half. Shape half into the tail to fit on the pointed end of the cake, then mould the other half into the head. Place the head and tail in position, moulding them on to the cake.

4 Colour about 500 g/1¼ lb/3¾ cups of the sugarpaste icing pink. Roll out on a surface lightly dusted with icing sugar to a long, thin rectangle. Brush the cake with the apricot glaze and cover with the icing. Smooth the sides and edges and trim.

5 To make the legs, colour 115 g/ 4 oz/¾ cup of the remaining icing orange. Set aside 25 g/1 oz/2 tbsp. Roll the remainder into ten balls the size of a walnut. Squeeze two balls together for each back leg and three for each front leg. Mark the toes with a fork. Brush with water and stick the legs in place.

6 Make one small and three large horns with the reserved orange icing, then stick in place with water. Colour 75 g/3 oz/½ cup of the remaining icing green and shape into cones. Stick on with water. Colour half the remaining icing black. Use the black and white icing to make the mouth, eyes and eyebrows.

Dumper Truck

Any large round biscuits will work well for the wheels and all sorts of coloured sweets can go into the truck.

Serves 8–10

INGREDIENTS

1½ x quantity Quick-mix Sponge Cake mix*
90 ml/6 tbsp Apricot Glaze*
2⅔ x quantity Sugarpaste Icing*
yellow, red and blue food colouring
about 12 sandwich wafer biscuits
4 coconut swirl biscuits
115 g/4 oz coloured sweets
5 cm/2 in piece blue liquorice stick
demerara sugar, for the sand
* See Basic Cakes, Icings & Glazes

1 Preheat the oven to 180°C/350°F/Gas 4. Grease and line a 900 g/2 lb/5 cup loaf tin. Spoon the cake mixture into the tin, smooth the surface and bake for 40–45 minutes, until a metal skewer inserted into the centre comes out clean. Transfer to a wire rack to cool.

2 Cut off the top of the cake. Cut off one-third of the cake for the cabin. Holding the larger piece cut side up, cut a hollow in the centre, leaving a 1 cm/½ in border. Brush with glaze.

3 Colour 350 g/12 oz/2¼ cups of the icing yellow. Set aside a piece the size of a walnut. Roll out the remainder on a surface lightly dusted with icing sugar to 5 mm/¼ in thick. Use to cover the larger piece of cake, pressing it into the hollow. Trim the bottom edges.

4 Colour 350 g/12 oz/2¼ cups of the remaining icing red. Set aside one-third and roll out the remainder to 5 mm/¼ in thick. Brush the remaining piece of cake with glaze, cover with the icing and trim the edges.

5 Break off and set aside a piece of the reserved red icing the size of a walnut and roll out the remainder. Brush an 18 x 7.5 cm/7 x 3 in piece of cake card with glaze and cover with the icing.

6 Brush the wafers with glaze and stick together in two equal piles. Place them on a 30 x 18 cm/12 x 7 in cake board about 7.5 cm/3 in apart. Place the covered cake card on top.

7 Place a little of the remaining white icing about halfway along the card. Place the dumper, slightly tilted, on top and the red cabin in front. Stand the coconut biscuits in position for wheels.

8 Roll out the reserved yellow icing to a 5 x 2.5 cm/2 x 1 in rectangle. Colour the remaining icing blue and roll out thinly. Stamp out eyes with a crescent cutter. Roll out the reserved red icing and stamp out a mouth. Stick the yellow panel to the front of the cabin with a little water and stick on the features. Fill the dumper with sweets and push a piece of liquorice into the top of the cabin. Scatter the sugar around the truck to make sand.

Lion Cake

This spectacular cake is surprisingly easy to make and would be perfect for an animal lover or a Leo.

Serves 10–15

INGREDIENTS
1½ x quantity Quick-mix Sponge Cake mix*
1 quantity orange-flavoured Butter Icing*
orange and red food colouring
1½ x quantity yellow Marzipan*
⅙ quantity Sugarpaste Icing*
red or orange liquorice bootlaces
long and round marshmallows
* See Basic Cakes, Icings & Glazes

1 Preheat the oven to 180°C/350°F/Gas 4. Grease and line a 25 x 30 cm/10 x 12 in tin. Spoon in the cake mixture, smooth the top and bake for 45–50 minutes, until a metal skewer inserted into the centre comes out clean. Leave in the tin for 5 minutes, then turn out on to a wire rack.

2 Place the cake base side up and cut an uneven scallop design around the edge. Turn the cake over and trim the top so that it sits squarely. Place it on a 30 cm/12 in square cake board.

3 Colour the butter icing orange and spread it evenly over the surface and down the sides of the cake.

4 Roll out about 115 g/4 oz/¾ cup of the marzipan on a surface lightly dusted with icing sugar to a 15 cm/6 in square. Place in the centre of the cake, gently pressing down to secure.

5 Grate the remaining marzipan on to greaseproof paper. With a palette knife, gently press it on to the cake to cover the sides and the top up to the edges of the face panel.

6 Colour the sugarpaste icing red and roll out on a surface lightly dusted with icing sugar. Stamp out a nose using a heart-shaped cutter and stick on the cake with a little water. With your fingers, roll two thin short strands for the mouth and stick on the cake.

7 Cut the liquorice bootlaces into lengths for the whiskers and place on the cake. Flatten two round marshmallows for eyes and stick on the cake with a little water. Cut the long marshmallows into 5 cm/2 in lengths and snip along one side to make the eyebrows. Stick on the cake with a little water.

Merry-go-round Cake

Choose your own figures to sit on the merry-go-round, from chocolate animals to jelly bears.

Serves 16–20

INGREDIENTS
1⅓ x quantity lemon-flavoured Quick-mix
    Sponge Cake mix*
60 ml/4 tbsp Apricot Glaze*
1⅔ x quantity Sugarpaste Icing*
orange and yellow food colouring
8 x 18 cm/7 in long candy sticks
sweet figures
* See Basic Cakes, Icings & Glazes

1 Preheat the oven to 180°C/350°F/ Gas 4. Grease and line two 20 cm/8 in round sandwich tins. Spoon two-thirds of the cake mixture into one tin and the rest into the other, smooth the top and bake for 30–60 minutes, until a metal skewer inserted into the centres comes out clean. Leave in the tins for 5 minutes, then turn on to a wire rack.

2 Place the larger cake upside down on a 23 cm/9 in round fluted cake board. Place the smaller cake right side up on an 18 cm/7 in round piece of stiff card. Brush both with the glaze.

3 Roll out 450 g/1 lb/3 cups of the icing on a surface dusted with icing sugar. Add a few spots of orange food colouring with a cocktail stick. Roll the icing into a sausage shape, fold in half and roll out to its original length. Repeat until it is streaked.

4 Roll out two-thirds of the orange icing and cover the larger cake. Roll out the remaining orange icing and cover the smaller cake. Trim and reserve the trimmings.

5 Using a candy stick, make eight holes evenly around the edge of the larger cake, leaving a 2 cm/¾ in border. Press the stick right through the cake to the board.

6 Knead the reserved orange icing until evenly coloured, then roll out thinly. Stamp out nine stars with a small star-shaped cutter and reserve.

7 Colour the remaining icing yellow. Roll it out and stamp out nine stars with a larger star-shaped cutter. Place the smaller cake on an upturned bowl and stick eight large and eight small stars around the edge with a little water. Stick the remaining stars on top.

8 Secure the sweet figures to the candy sticks with reserved icing trimmings. Leave them to set for 30 minutes. Place the candy sticks in the holes in the larger cake. Assemble the cake just before serving. Lift the smaller cake, with its card base, on to the candy sticks, making sure it balances before letting go.

Child's Fairy Cake

Allow yourself plenty of time for decorating this enchanting novelty cake.

Serves 6–8

INGREDIENTS
1 quantity Quick-mix Sponge Cake mix*
⅓ quantity Butter Icing*
30 ml/2 tbsp Apricot Glaze*
1 quantity Marzipan*
⅓ quantity Royal Icing*
pink sparkle lustre powder
silver balls

FOR THE FONDANT ICING
450 g/1 lb/4 cups icing sugar
1 egg white
27½ ml/5½ tsp liquid glucose
blue, pink, yellow and gold food colouring
* See Basic Cakes, Icings & Glazes

1 Preheat the oven to 160°C/325°F/ Gas 3. Grease and line a 20 cm/8 in round cake tin. Spoon in the mixture, smooth the surface and bake for 30–40 minutes, until a skewer inserted into the centre comes out clean. Turn out on to a wire rack to cool.

2 To make the fondant icing, put the icing sugar, egg white and glucose in a food processor or mixer and process until the mixture resembles fine breadcrumbs. Knead well until smooth and pliable, adding a drop of water if it is too dry. Set aside 50 g/2 oz/¼ cup in a plastic bag in the fridge and colour the remainder pale blue, kneading well.

3 Cut the cake in half horizontally and sandwich together with the butter icing. Place on a 25 cm/10 in round cake board and brush with the glaze. Roll out the marzipan and use to cover the cake. Roll out the blue fondant icing and use to cover the cake. Leave to dry overnight.

4 Using a template, mark the position of the fairy. Spoon the royal icing into a piping bag with a No. 1 nozzle and pipe the outline of each wing. Pipe a second line inside the first. With a damp paint brush, brush long strokes in from the edges, leaving more icing at the edges and fading away to a thin film near the base. Leave to dry for 1 hour. Brush with dry lustre powder.

5 Colour a little of the white fondant icing flesh colour. Roll out and cut out the body. Stick on the cake with a little water. Round sharp edges with your finger. Cut out the bodice and shoes and stick in place. Cut out a wand and star and leave to dry.

6 Make the tutu frills one at a time. Roll out a small piece of fondant to 3 mm/⅛ in thick and stamp out a circle with a small fluted cutter. Cut it into quarters and roll a wooden cocktail stick along the fluted edge to stretch it and give fullness.

7 Stick one frill to the waist. Repeat with the other layers, tucking the sides in neatly. Use a cocktail stick to arrange the frills and support the folds with small pieces of cotton wool until dry.

8 Brush a little lustre powder over the edge of the tutu. Paint on the hair and face, stick on the wand and star and paint the star gold. Pipe a border of royal icing around the board using a No. 7 star nozzle and place a silver ball on alternate points. Leave to dry.

9 Colour a little royal icing yellow and pipe over the hair. Paint with a touch of gold colouring.

Indian Elephant

You can also make this delightful pachyderm for someone who loves to travel. Be as colourful as you like with the decoration.

Serves 30

INGREDIENTS
1¾ x quantity Madeira Cake mix*
2 x quantity Butter Icing*
½ quantity Marzipan*
black, green, yellow and pink
   food colouring
chocolate coins
silver balls
brown and white
   chocolate buttons
2 flat, round-shaped sweets
115 g/4 oz/2 cups
   desiccated coconut
30 ml/2 tbsp Apricot Glaze*
* See Basic Cakes, Icings & Glazes

1 Preheat the oven to 160°C/325°F/ Gas 3. Grease and line a 30 cm/12 in square cake tin. Spoon in the mixture, tap lightly to level the surface and bake for 1½ hours, until a metal skewer inserted into the centre comes out clean. Place the tin on a wire rack for 10 minutes, then turn the cake out on to the rack to cool.

2 Make a template from stiff paper in the shape of an elephant and place on top of the cake. Cut out the shape with a sharp knife and transfer to a 35 cm/14 in cake board.

3 Colour the icing pale grey and cover the top and sides of the cake. Swirl with a palette knife. Swirl black food colouring highlights into the icing with a cocktail stick.

4 Roll out half the marzipan on a surface lightly dusted with icing sugar. Cut out shapes for the tusk, headpiece and blanket. Colour the remaining marzipan green, yellow and pink. Roll and cut out patterns for the blanket, headpiece, trunk and tail. Roll small balls of yellow and pink marzipan for the anklets.

5 Place the patterns and decorations in position. Cut the white chocolate buttons in half for toenails and make an eye from the sweets.

6 Colour the desiccated coconut green. Brush the cake board with the apricot glaze and sprinkle with the coconut.

29

Flickering Candle Cake

Stripy icing candles are flickering and ready to blow out on this birthday celebration cake for all ages.

Serves 15–20

INGREDIENTS
1⅓ x quantity Madeira Cake mix*
1 quantity Butter Icing*
45 ml/3 tbsp Apricot Glaze*
2½ x quantity Sugarpaste Icing*
pink, yellow, purple and jade
   food colouring
edible silver balls
edible-ink pens
* See Basic Cakes, Icings & Glazes

1 Preheat the oven to 160°C/325°F/Gas 3. Grease and line a 20 cm/8 in square cake tin. Spoon in the mixture, tap the tin lightly to level and bake for 1¼–1½ hours, until a metal skewer inserted into the centre comes out clean. Place the tin on a wire rack for 10 minutes, then turn the cake out on to the rack to cool.

2 Cut the cake horizontally into three layers. Sandwich the layers together with the butter icing and brush the cake with the apricot glaze. Roll out 500 g/1¼ lb/3¾ cups of the sugarpaste icing on a surface lightly dusted with icing sugar. Use the sugarpaste icing to cover the cake completely and trim the edges neatly. Place the cake on a 23 cm/9 in square cake board.

3 Divide the remaining icing into quarters and colour them pink, yellow, purple and jade. Roll out the jade icing and cut into six 1 cm/½ in strips of unequal length, but each long enough to go up the side and on to the top of the cake. Make a diagonal cut at one end of each. Roll out the yellow icing and stamp out six flames with a leaf-shaped cutter. Place a silver ball in each flame.

4 Stick the candles on the cake with a little water. Mould small strips, fractionally longer than the candles' width, from the yellow and purple icing. Stick alternate colour strips on the candles at a slight angle. Stick the flames at the top.

5 Roll out the pink icing and the remaining purple icing and cut out wavy pieces. Stick on the cake above the candles. Gather the pink trimmings into a ball.

6 Roll out the remaining yellow icing and stamp out circles with a small round cutter or the end of a piping nozzle. Make small balls from the remaining pink icing and stick them to the yellow circles. Press a silver ball into the centre of each decoration. Stick the decorations around the bottom of the cake.

7 Draw wavy lines and dots coming from the purple and pink wavy icing with food colouring pens. Decorate the sides of the cake board with jade ribbon, securing it with a little softened sugar paste.

Birthday Parcel

Here is a birthday cake that is all wrapped up and ready to eat. Change the pattern by using different shaped cutters.

Serves 10

INGREDIENTS
⅔ quantity Madeira Cake mix*
¾ quantity orange-flavour Butter Icing*
45 ml/3 tbsp apricot jam, warmed
   and sieved
1⅓ x quantity Sugarpaste Icing*
blue, orange and green food colouring
* See Basic Cakes, Icings & Glazes

1 Preheat the oven to 160°C/325°F/
Gas 3. Grease and line a 15 cm/6 in
square cake tin. Spoon in the mixture,
tap to level it and bake for 1 hour
10 minutes, or until a metal skewer
inserted into the centre comes out
clean. Place the tin on a wire rack for
10 minutes, then turn the cake out on
to the rack to cool completely.

2 Cut the cake in half horizontally
and sandwich together with the butter
icing. Brush the cake with the jam.
Colour three-quarters of the
sugarpaste icing blue. Divide the
remaining icing in half and colour one
half orange and the other green.

3 Roll out the blue icing on a surface
lightly dusted with icing sugar and use
it to cover the cake. Place on the cake
board. Stamp out circles and triangles
from the icing with cocktail cutters,
lifting out to expose the cake.

4 Roll out the orange and green
icing and stamp out circles and
triangles. Fill the holes in the blue
icing with the orange and green
shapes. Gather the trimmings to use
for the ribbons.

5 Roll out the orange trimmings and
cut three strips about 2 cm/¾ in wide
and long enough to go over each
corner of the cake. Roll out the green
trimmings and cut three very thin
strips the same length as the orange
ones. Place the orange and green strips
next to each other to give three
striped ribbons and stick together with
a little water.

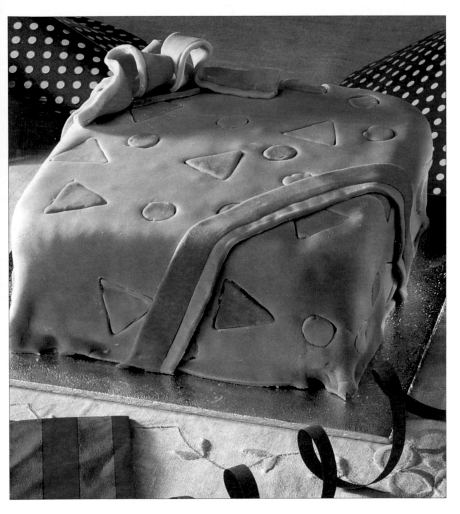

6 Stick one striped ribbon over one corner of the cake. Stick a second strip over the opposite corner. Cut the remaining ribbon in half. Bend each half to make loops and stick both to the ribbon over one corner of the cake to form a loose bow.

Eighteenth Birthday Cake

A really striking and sophisticated cake for a lucky someone celebrating their eighteenth birthday.

Serves 80

INGREDIENTS
1⅓ x quantity Light Fruit Cake mix*
45 ml/3 tbsp Apricot Glaze*
2½ x quantity Marzipan*
4⅔ x quantity Sugarpaste Icing*
black food colouring
30 ml/2 tbsp Royal Icing*
* See Basic Cakes, Icings & Glazes

1 Preheat the oven to 150°C/300°F/ Gas 2. Grease and line a 33.5 x 20 cm/ 13½ x 8 in diamond-shaped deep cake tin. Spoon in the mixture, smooth the top, make a slight dip in the centre and bake for 3¼–3¾ hours, until a metal skewer put into the centre comes out clean. Cool in the tin, then turn out.

2 Brush the cake with glaze and place it on a cake board. Roll out the marzipan on a surface lightly dusted with icing sugar. Use to cover the cake and trim the edges.

3 Roll out 1.1 kg/2½ lb/3⅓ cups of the sugarpaste icing on a surface lightly dusted with icing sugar and use to cover the cake, trimming the edges. Knead the trimmings into the remaining sugarpaste and colour it black. Roll out two-thirds and cut into four strips the width and length of each section of the cake board.

4 Brush the board with glaze, place each strip in position and trim. Roll out one-quarter of the remaining sugarpaste and stamp out the number 18 with a special cutter or using a template. Leave on a piece of foam sponge to dry. Roll out some more sugarpaste and use a cocktail cutter to stamp out 40 triangles for the bow ties and 20 for the glasses.

5 Roll out some more sugarpaste and stamp out 20 circles for the music notes and 10 bases for the glasses with a tiny round cutter. Cut the bases in half. Cut out thin strips for the tails of the notes and the stems of the glasses.

6 Colour the royal icing black and spoon into a piping bag fitted with a No. 1 plain writing nozzle. With tiny beads of icing, join the bow ties together, attach the music notes to their tails and the glasses to their stems and bases. Leave to dry.

7 Arrange the numbers, notes, glasses and bow ties over the top of the cake, then stick them down with a bead of icing. Finish the decoration with black and white ribbons.

Twenty-first Birthday Cake

This cake looks good in any pale colour or simply white. Add the colour with the ribbons and write your own message.

Serves 80

INGREDIENTS
1⅔ x quantity Light Fruit
   Cake mix*
45 ml/3 tbsp Apricot Glaze*
2½ x quantity Marzipan*
2 x quantity Royal Icing*
blue food colouring
500 g/1¼ lb ready-made
   petal paste
cornflour, for dusting
* See Basic Cakes, Icings & Glazes

1 Preheat the oven to 150°C/300°F/ Gas 2. Grease and line a 25 cm/10 in round deep cake tin. Spoon in the mixture, smooth the top, make a slight depression in the centre and bake for 3¾ hours, until a metal skewer inserted into the centre comes out clean. Cool in the tin, then turn out.

2 Brush the cake with glaze and place on a 30 cm/12 in round cake board. Roll out the marzipan on a surface lightly dusted with icing sugar. Use to cover the cake and trim the edges.

3 Colour the royal icing pale blue. Flat-ice the top and side of the cake with three layers of smooth royal icing, leaving each to dry before adding the next, then ice the cake board.

4 Colour the petal paste pale blue. Roll out one-third on a surface lightly dusted with cornflour. Stamp out two squares with a 7.5 cm/3 in fluted cutter. Stamp out an oval from one square with a 5 cm/2 in plain cutter. Make two tiny holes with a No. 2 plain writing nozzle on the left hand edge on both squares to match. Continue to make a cut-out pattern all around the front of the card. Leave on a piece of foam sponge to dry.

5 Roll out some more petal paste. Stamp out 25 shapes with a club-shaped cocktail cutter, allowing for breakage. Use a tiny petal cutter to cut out three shapes on each piece. Leave to dry thoroughly. Roll out the remaining paste and stamp out two end shapes for the keys with the club cutter. Cut out the remaining parts of the key shapes with a sharp knife. Pattern the keys with tiny cutters. Leave to dry.

6 Tie plain pale and royal blue ribbons around the board, securing with a pin. Fit looped royal blue ribbon around the side of the cake and secure with a bead of icing.

7 Spoon blue icing into a piping bag fitted with a No. 3 plain writing nozzle. Arrange 18 cut-out sugar pieces around the top edge of the cake and secure with a bead of icing. Leave to dry. Pipe a shell edging around the base and between the cut-outs on top.

8 Write your message on the plain card with a food colouring pen and decorate the keys. Thread narrow royal blue ribbon around the card and through the matching holes to join it. Tie in a bow with long ends.

9 Thread matching ribbon through the cut-out sugar pieces, joining the ends with a bead of icing. Tie a bow and stick it to the side of the cake with a bead of icing. Attach the card and the keys with icing and leave to dry.

Flower Birthday Cake

Pretty piped sugar flowers and coral and white ribbons decorate this charming birthday cake.

Serves 40

INGREDIENTS
¾ quantity Light Fruit Cake mix*
30 ml/2 tbsp Apricot Glaze*
1½ x quantity Marzipan*
3¾ x quantity Royal Icing*
yellow and orange food colouring
* See Basic Cakes, Icings & Glazes

1 Preheat the oven to 150°C/300°F/ Gas 2. Grease and line a 18 cm/7 in round deep cake tin. Spoon in the mixture, smooth the top, make a slight depression in the centre and bake for 2½–2¾ hours, until a metal skewer inserted into the centre comes out clean. Cool in the tin, then turn out.

2 Brush the cake with the glaze. Roll out the marzipan on a surface lightly dusted with icing sugar and use to cover the cake. Transfer to a 23 cm/ 9 in round cake board. Flat-ice the top and side of the cake with three layers of royal icing, leaving each to dry, then ice the cake board.

3 Snip an inverted V shape off the point of a greaseproof paper piping bag. Fit another bag with a petal nozzle, a third with a No. 1 plain writing nozzle and a fourth with a medium star nozzle.

4 Colour one-third of the remaining icing yellow and then colour 15 ml/ 1 tbsp of the icing orange. Pipe the narcissi using the petal nozzle for the petals and the writing nozzle for the centres. Make four white narcissi with yellow centres and nine yellow narcissi with orange centres.

5 Pipe nine simple white flowers with the snipped bag and add yellow centres with the plain nozzle. Leave to dry on greaseproof paper.

6 Arrange the flowers on the top of the cake, securing them with a little icing. With white icing and a star nozzle, pipe shell edging all around the top and base of the cake.

7 With white icing and a No. 2 plain writing nozzle, pipe "Happy Birthday" on either side of the flowers.

8 Place white ribbon around the board and secure with a pin. Place coral ribbon around the board and side of the cake, securing with a bead of icing. Over-pipe the writing with orange icing and a No. 1 plain writing nozzle. Tie a bow and stick to the cake with a bead of icing. Leave to dry.

Birthday Bowl of Strawberries

With its hand-painted picture and moulded fruit, this is the ideal cake to celebrate a summer birthday.

Serves 20

INGREDIENTS
1 quantity Madeira Cake mix*
1 quantity Butter Icing*
45 ml/3 tbsp Apricot Glaze*
2 x quantity Sugarpaste Icing*
pink, red, yellow, green and claret
   food colouring
cornflour, for dusting
yellow powdered food colouring
* See Basic Cakes, Icings & Glazes

1 Preheat the oven to 160°C/325°F/ Gas 3. Grease and line a 20 cm/8 in petal-shaped cake tin. Spoon in the mixture, tap lightly to level and bake for 1¼ hours, until a metal skewer inserted into the centre comes out clean. Place the tin on a wire rack for 10 minutes, then turn the cake out on to the rack to cool.

2 Colour the butter icing pink. Cut the cake horizontally into three and sandwich together with the butter icing. Brush with the glaze. Roll out 500g/1¼ lb/3¾ cups of the sugarpaste icing on a surface that has been lightly dusted with icing sugar. Use to cover the cake and trim. Place the cake on a 25 cm/10 in petal-shaped cake board and leave to dry for 12 hours.

3 Colour three-quarters of the remaining sugarpaste red. Divide the rest in half and colour one half yellow and the other green. Dust your hands with cornflour and mould the red icing into strawberries.

4 Make tiny oval shapes from the yellow icing and press on to the strawberries. Shape the green icing into flat circles and snip round the edges with scissors. Curl the edges slightly and stick to the top of the strawberries with a little water. Leave to dry on greaseproof paper.

5 Put red, green, yellow and claret food colouring on a palette and dilute slightly with a little water. Paint the outline of the bowl with the claret food colouring, then fill in the pattern. Add highlights with a little of the yellow powdered food colouring.

6 Finish painting the pattern, filling in the strawberries in the bowl and around the edge of the cake.

7 Decorate the cake with red and green ribbons. Stick two moulded strawberries to the top and arrange the others around the bottom.

Frosted Flower Cake

If pansies are not in season, use other edible flowers – just co-ordinate the colour of the icing and decoration.

Serves 20–25

INGREDIENTS
1 quantity Light Fruit Cake mix*
45 ml/3 tbsp Apricot Glaze*
1½ x quantity Marzipan*
1⅔ x quantity Royal Icing*
orange food colouring
about 7 orange and
    purple pansies
1 egg white, lightly beaten
caster sugar, for frosting
* See Basic Cakes, Icings & Glazes

1 Preheat the oven to 150°C/300°F/ Gas 2. Grease and line a 20 cm/8 in round deep cake tin. Spoon in the mixture, smooth the top, make a slight depression in the centre and bake for 2¾–3¼ hours, until a metal skewer inserted into the centre comes out clean. Cool in the tin, then turn out.

2 Brush the cake with the glaze. Roll out the marzipan on a surface lightly dusted with icing sugar and use to cover the cake.

3 Secure the cake to a 25 cm/10 in round cake board with a little icing. Colour one-quarter of the icing pale orange. Flat-ice the cake with three or four layers of icing, using orange for the top and white for the sides. Leave each layer to dry.

4 Wash the pansies and dry on kitchen paper. Leave a short piece of stem attached. Brush both sides of the petals with egg white. Holding the flowers by the stems, sprinkle them evenly with sugar, then shake off the excess. Leave to dry on a wire rack covered with greaseproof paper.

5 Spoon some white icing into a piping bag fitted with a No. 19 star nozzle. Pipe a row of scrolls around the top of the cake. Pipe a second row of scrolls in the opposite direction, directly underneath. Pipe another row of scrolls around the bottom of the cake.

6 Spoon some orange icing into a piping bag fitted with a No. 1 writing nozzle. Pipe around the outline of the top of each scroll. Pipe a row of orange dots under the reverse scrolls and a double row of dots above the bottom row of scrolls. Arrange the pansies on top of the cake. Decorate with a wide and a narrow purple ribbon.

43

Cloth of Roses Cake

It is almost too pretty to eat, so make this for a very special birthday.

Serves 20–25

INGREDIENTS
1 quantity Light Fruit Cake mix*
45 ml/3 tbsp Apricot Glaze*
1½ x quantity Marzipan*
2⅔ x quantity Sugarpaste Icing*
yellow, orange and green food colouring
cornflour, for dusting
⅙ quantity Royal Icing*
* See Basic Cakes, Icings & Glazes

1 Preheat the oven to 150°C/300°F/ Gas 2. Grease and line a 20 cm/8 in round deep cake tin. Spoon in the mixture, smooth the top, make a slight depression in the centre and bake for 2¾–3¼ hours, until a metal skewer inserted into the centre comes out clean. Cool in the tin, then turn out.

2 Brush the cake with the glaze. Roll out the marzipan on a surface lightly dusted with icing sugar and use to cover the cake. Cut out a template from greaseproof paper: draw a 25 cm/ 10 in circle. Use a 7 cm/2¾ in plain cutter as a guide to draw half circles 2.5 cm/1 in wide all around the outside of the large circle. Cut out.

3 Colour 350 g/12 oz/2¼ cups of the sugarpaste pale yellow and roll out on a work surface lightly dusted with icing sugar. Use to cover the cake. Place the cake on a 25 cm/10 in cake board.

4 Colour 350 g/12 oz/2¼ cups of the remaining sugarpaste pale orange and roll out to a 30 cm/12 in circle. Place the template on the icing and cut out. Brush the cake with water and cover with the orange icing so that the scallops fall just over the edge. Curl them slightly and leave to dry.

5 Reserve about one-quarter of the remaining sugarpaste for the leaves and divide the rest into quarters. Colour them pale yellow, deep yellow, orange and marbled yellow and orange.

6 Dust your hands with cornflour. To make the roses, take a small ball of sugarpaste and form into a cone. Form a piece into a petal slightly thicker at the base. Press around the cone, so it sits above the top. Curl the end.

7 Repeat with several more petals, making them slightly larger each time and attaching them so they just overlap. Cut off the base. Make about 18 roses and dry on greaseproof paper.

8 Colour the remaining sugarpaste green. Roll out thinly and stamp out about 24 leaves with a petal cutter. Leave to dry on greaseproof paper.

9 Arrange the leaves and roses on the cake, securing them with a bead of royal icing. Decorate the cake with a thin yellow ribbon.

45

Celebration Rose and Fruit Cake

Covered with delicately flavoured rose water icing, this luscious cake is decorated with frosted roses.

Serves 20–25

INGREDIENTS
1 quantity Light Fruit Cake mix*
900 g/2 lb/5½ cups icing sugar
3 egg whites
5 ml/1 tsp distilled rose water
2.5 ml/½ tsp lemon juice
120 ml/4 fl oz/½ cup
   liquid glucose
45 ml/3 tbsp rose jelly
8–9 roses
caster sugar, for frosting
* See Basic Cakes, Icings & Glazes

1 Preheat the oven to 150°C/300°F/ Gas 2. Grease and line a 20 cm/8 in round deep cake tin. Spoon in the mixture, smooth the top, make a slight depression into the centre and bake for 2¾–3¼ hours, until a metal skewer inserted into the centre comes out clean. Cool in the tin, then turn out.

2 Sift the icing sugar into a bowl and beat in two of the egg whites, the rose water, lemon juice and liquid glucose with a wooden spoon. Knead until the mixture forms a smooth, pliable icing.

3 Transfer the cake to a 25 cm/10 in round cake board. Brush the top and side with the rose jelly, warming it first, if necessary. Roll out the icing on a surface lightly dusted with icing sugar. Position the icing on the cake, smoothing the top and the sides. Frill out at the base of the cake and trim off any excess.

4 Wash the roses and dry on kitchen paper. Leave a little of the stem still attached. Lightly beat the remaining egg white. Brush both sides of the rose petals with the egg white. Holding the flowers by the stems, sprinkle them evenly with sugar, then shake off the excess. Leave to dry on a wire rack covered with greaseproof paper.

5 If necessary, trim the stems of the roses. Arrange three roses on top of the cake and the remainder around the frill at the base.

Tía Maria Gâteau

Whipped cream and Tía Maria make a mouthwatering filling for this light chocolate and walnut cake.

Serves 6–8

INGREDIENTS
150 g/5 oz/1¼ cups self-raising flour
25 g/1 oz/¼ cup cocoa powder
7.5 ml/1½ tsp baking powder
3 eggs, beaten
175 g/6 oz/¾ cup butter, softened
175 g/6 oz/scant 1 cup
   caster sugar
50 g/2 oz/½ cup chopped walnuts
walnut brittle, to decorate

FOR THE FILLING AND COATING
600 ml/1 pint/2½ cups double cream
45 ml/3 tbsp Tía Maria
50 g/2 oz/⅔ cup desiccated
   coconut, toasted

1 Preheat the oven to 160°C/325°F/ Gas 3. Lightly grease and base-line two 18 cm/7 in sandwich tins. Sift the flour, cocoa powder and baking powder into a large bowl. Add the eggs, butter, sugar and chopped walnuts and mix together thoroughly.

2 Divide the mixture between the cake tins, smooth the surface and bake for 35–40 minutes, until risen and golden. Turn out the cakes on to a wire rack and leave to cool.

3 For the filling, add the Tía Maria to the cream and whisk until the mixture forms soft peaks.

4 Slice each cake horizontally in half to give four layers. Sandwich the layers together with some of the flavoured cream and use some more to coat the side of the cake.

COOK'S TIP: To make walnut brittle, heat 75 g/3 oz/6 tbsp caster sugar in a pan. When the sugar has melted, stir in 50 g/2 oz/½ cup broken walnuts. Turn the mixture on to non-stick baking parchment and leave to set. Break the brittle into pieces with a rolling pin.

5 Spread out the toasted coconut on a sheet of non-stick baking parchment. Then, holding the top and bottom of the cake, roll the side in the coconut until evenly coated. Put the cake on a serving plate, spread more of the cream on top and pipe the remainder around the outside rim. Decorate inside the rim with walnut brittle.

Pineapple & Kirsch Cake

A dramatic effect is created when this cake, with its kirsch-flavoured creamy filling, is sliced to reveal the striped pattern inside.

Serves 10–12

INGREDIENTS
175 g/6 oz/¾ cup butter
115 g/4 oz/½ cup caster sugar, plus extra
  for sprinkling
2 eggs, lightly beaten
115 g/4 oz/1 cup self-raising flour, sifted
10 ml/2 tsp grated lemon rind
225 g/8 oz ginger biscuits, crushed
pineapple wedges and leaves, to decorate

FOR THE FILLING AND COATING
750 ml/1¼ pints/3 cups double cream,
  whipped
30 ml/2 tbsp kirsch
225 g/8 oz fresh pineapple, finely chopped
115 g/4 oz/1⅓ cups desiccated coconut,
  toasted

1 Preheat the oven to 200°C/400°F/ Gas 6. Grease and line a 28 x 18 cm/ 11 x 7 in Swiss roll tin. Grease and line a 20 cm/8 in round springform cake tin. Put 50 g/2 oz/4 tbsp of the butter, the sugar, eggs, flour and lemon rind in a bowl and beat until light and fluffy. Spread the mixture in the Swiss roll tin and bake for 10–12 minutes, until firm and golden.

2 Meanwhile, melt the remaining butter in a pan and stir in the crushed biscuits. Press the crumb mixture over the base of the round cake tin.

3 When the cake is cooked, turn it out on to a sheet of non-stick baking parchment sprinkled with caster sugar. Remove the lining paper.

4 Make the filling and coating. Combine half of the whipped cream with the kirsch and the chopped pineapple. Spread the mixture over the cake and then cut the cake into four long strips.

5 Roll up the first strip of cake and filling and stand it on one end in the tin on the biscuit base. Wrap the remaining strips around to form a 20 cm/8 in cake. Chill for 15 minutes.

6 Carefully remove the cake from the tin and place it on a serving plate. Spoon some of the remaining cream into a piping bag and spread the rest over top and side of the cake. Cover with toasted coconut. Pipe swirls of cream on top of the cake and decorate with pineapple wedges and leaves.

COOK'S TIP: Give a marbled effect to the cake by colouring half the sponge mixture with a few drops of food colouring. Put alternate spoonfuls of plain and tinted into the tin and swirl with a skewer before baking.

Caramel Meringue Gâteau with Sloe Gin

Two crisp rounds of orange meringue are filled with a refreshing blend of cream, mango, grapes and sloe gin.

Serves 8

INGREDIENTS
4 egg whites
225 g/8 oz/1 cup light
   brown sugar
3 drops of white wine vinegar
3 drops of vanilla essence
10 ml/2 tsp grated orange rind
whipped cream, to decorate

FOR THE FILLING AND
   CARAMEL TOPPING
300 ml/½ pint/1¼ cups
   double cream
45 ml/3 tbsp sloe gin
1 mango, chopped
225 g/8 oz mixed green and black
   seedless grapes, halved
75 g/3 oz/6 tbsp granulated sugar

1 Preheat the oven to 160°C/325°F/ Gas 3. Base-line two 20 cm/8 in sandwich tins. Whisk the egg whites until stiff. Add half the sugar and continue to whisk until the meringue softens again.

2 Fold in the remaining sugar, the white wine vinegar, vanilla essence and grated orange rind. Divide the mixture between the tins, spread evenly and bake for 40 minutes. Leave to cool.

3 Make the filling. Whip the double cream in a large bowl until it is fairly thick, then carefully fold in the sloe gin, chopped mango and halved green and black grapes using a wooden spoon.

4 Gently spread one meringue layer with the whipped cream and fruit mixture, then place the second meringue layer on top of the filling and press it down firmly but carefully, so that the delicate meringue does not break. Transfer the gâteau to a serving plate.

5 Line a baking sheet with non-stick baking parchment. Put the sugar for the caramel topping into a heavy-based pan. Heat gently until it melts. Increase the heat and cook, without stirring, until it becomes golden and a spoonful hardens when dropped into cold water.

6 Drizzle some of the caramel on to the baking parchment to make decorative shapes and allow these to cool and harden. Drizzle the remaining caramel over the gâteau. Decorate the top with the whipped cream and stand the cooled caramel shapes upright in the cream.

Jazzy Chocolate Gâteau

With its modern and sophisticated appearance, this would make a good birthday cake for a teenager.

Serves 12–15

INGREDIENTS
2 x quantity chocolate-flavoured Quick-mix
    Sponge Mix*
75 g/3 oz plain chocolate
75 g/3 oz white chocolate
½ quantity Fudge Frosting*
120 ml/8 tbsp chocolate
    hazelnut spread
* See Basic Cakes, Icings & Glazes

FOR THE COFFEE GLACE ICING
115 g/4 oz/1 cup icing sugar
5 ml/1 tsp weak coffee
30 ml/2 tbsp warm water

1 Preheat the oven to 160°C/325°F/Gas 3. Grease and line two 20 cm/8 in round cake tins. Divide the cake mixture equally between the tins, smooth the surfaces and bake for 20–30 minutes, until a metal skewer inserted into the centres comes out clean. Turn out on to a wire rack.

2 Meanwhile, cover a large baking sheet with baking parchment. Melt the plain and white chocolate in separate bowls over pans of simmering water, stirring until smooth, then pour on to the baking sheet.

3 Spread out evenly with a palette knife and leave to cool until firm enough to cut. When the chocolate no longer feels sticky, cut out random shapes and set aside.

4 Sandwich the two cooled cakes together with the fudge frosting and transfer to a serving plate.

5 To make the icing, sift the sugar into a bowl, stir in the coffee and gradually stir in sufficient water to give the consistency of thick cream. Beat until smooth. Spread the icing on top of the cake almost to the edges.

6 Spread the side of the cake with enough chocolate hazelnut spread to cover. Arrange the chocolate pieces around the side of the cake, pressing them into the spread. Spoon about 45 ml/3 tbsp of the spread into a piping bag fitted with a No. 1 plain nozzle and pipe "jazzy" lines over the icing.

Divine Chocolate Cake

This very rich cake would be the best possible way to say "Happy Birthday" to a chocoholic.

Serves 18–20

INGREDIENTS
225 g/8 oz fine quality bittersweet
    chocolate, chopped
115 g/4 oz/½ cup unsalted butter,
    cut into pieces
170 ml/5½ fl oz/⅔ cup water
250 g/9 oz/1¼ cups
    granulated sugar
10 ml/2 tsp vanilla essence
2 eggs, separated
170 ml/5½ fl oz/⅔ cup buttermilk or
    soured cream
365 g/12½ oz/2 cups plain flour
10 ml/2 tsp baking powder
5 ml/1 tsp bicarbonate of soda
pinch of cream of tartar
chocolate curls, raspberries and icing
    sugar, to decorate

FOR THE CHOCOLATE FUDGE FILLING
450 g/1 lb fine quality couverture
    chocolate or bittersweet
    chocolate, chopped
225 g/8 oz/1 cup unsalted butter
75 ml/3 fl oz/⅓ cup brandy or rum
215 g/7½ oz/¾ cup seedless
    raspberry preserve

FOR THE CHOCOLATE GANACHE GLAZE
250 ml/8 fl oz/1 cup double cream
225 g/8 oz couverture chocolate or
    bittersweet chocolate, chopped
30 ml/2 tbsp brandy or rum

1 Preheat the oven to 180°C/350°F/ Gas 4. Grease and line a 25 cm/10 in springform tin.

2 Heat the chocolate, butter and water in a small saucepan, stirring frequently, until smooth. Remove from the heat, transfer to a bowl, beat in the sugar and cool. Lightly beat the egg yolks, then beat into the chocolate mixture with the vanilla essence.

3 Fold in the buttermilk or soured cream. Sift the flour, baking powder and bicarbonate of soda into a bowl, then fold into the chocolate mixture. Beat the egg whites and cream of tartar with an electric mixer until stiff peaks form, then fold into the chocolate mixture.

4 Pour the mixture into the tin and bake for 45–50 minutes, until the cake begins to shrink from the side of the tin. Place the tin on a wire rack for 10 minutes, then turn the cake out on to the rack to cool.

5 To make the filling, heat the chocolate, butter and 60 ml/4 tbsp of the brandy or rum in a saucepan, stirring frequently, until smooth. Remove from the heat and leave to cool and thicken.

6 Cut the cake horizontally into three layers. Heat the raspberry preserve and remaining brandy or rum, stirring frequently until smooth. Spread thinly over each layer and leave to set.

7 Place the bottom layer in the cleaned tin. Spread with half the filling, top with the second layer and spread with the remaining filling. Top with the final layer, coated side down.

8 Gently press together, cover and chill for 4–6 hours or overnight. Remove the cake from the tin and set on a wire rack over a tray.

9 To make the glaze, bring the cream to the boil in a pan. Remove from the heat, add all the chocolate and stir until smooth. Stir in the brandy or rum, strain and set aside for 4–5 minutes to thicken. Whisk until smooth and shiny.

10 Pour the glaze over the cake, smoothing with a palette knife. Leave to set, then transfer to a serving plate and decorate with chocolate curls and raspberries. Dust with icing sugar.

Chocolate Box with Caramel Mousse & Berries

Do not add the caramel shards too long before serving as moisture may cause them dissolve.

Serves 8–10

INGREDIENTS
275 g/10 oz semi-sweet chocolate broken
   into pieces

FOR THE CARAMEL MOUSSE
4 x 50 g/2 oz chocolate-coated caramel bars,
   coarsely chopped
20 ml/4 tsp milk or water
350 ml/12 fl oz/1½ cups double cream
1 egg white

FOR THE CARAMEL SHARDS
120 ml/8 tbsp granulated sugar
50 ml/2 fl oz/¼ cup water

FOR THE TOPPING
115 g/4 oz white chocolate, chopped
350 ml/12 fl oz/1½ cups
   double cream
450 g/1 lb mixed berries or cut-up fruits,
   such as raspberries, strawberries and
   blackberries or sliced nectarine and
   orange segments

1 To make the box, line a 23 cm/9 in baking tin with foil. Melt the semi-sweet chocolate in a bowl over a pan of simmering water, stirring constantly until smooth. Pour into the tin and keep tilting to coat the base and sides evenly. Chill for 45 minutes, until firm.

2 To make the mousse, put the caramel bars and milk or water in a bowl set over a pan of simmering water and stir until melted. Remove from the heat and cool for 10 minutes, stirring occasionally. Whip the cream with an electric mixer until soft peaks form. Stir a spoonful of the cream into the caramel mixture, then fold in the rest. In a separate bowl, beat the egg white until just stiff, then fold it into the mousse. Pour into the chocolate box and chill for 6–8 hours or overnight.

3 To make the caramel shards, lightly oil a baking sheet. Dissolve the sugar in the water over low heat, stirring gently, then boil for 4–5 minutes, until the mixture turns pale gold. Immediately pour on to the oiled sheet, tilting to spread evenly. Do not touch the hot caramel. Cool, then lift off the sheet and break into pieces with a metal palette knife. Set aside.

4 For the topping, heat the white chocolate with 120 ml/4 fl oz/½ cup cream over a low heat, stirring frequently, until smooth. Strain and leave to cool, stirring occasionally. Beat the remaining cream with an electric mixer until firm peaks form. Stir a spoonful of cream into the chocolate mixture, then fold in the remainder.

5 Remove the mousse-filled box from the foil by peeling it carefully from the sides and the base. Slide on to a serving plate. Spoon the chocolate-cream mixture into a piping bag fitted with a medium star nozzle and pipe rosettes or shells over the surface of the mousse. Decorate with fruits and caramel shards.

White Chocolate Cake

Make this superb cake for an extra special birthday, such as a fiftieth.

Serves 40–50

INGREDIENTS
FOR THE TWO CAKES
2 x 600 g/1 lb 5 oz/4 cups plain flour
2 x 10 ml/2 tsp bicarbonate of soda
2 x pinch of salt
2 x 225 g/8 oz white chocolate, chopped
2 x 250 ml/8 fl oz/1 cup whipping cream
2 x 225 g/8 oz/1 cup unsalted butter, softened
2 x 400 g/14 oz/2 cups caster sugar
2 x 6 eggs
2 x 10 ml/2 tsp lemon essence
2 x grated rind of 1 lemon
2 x 325 ml/11 fl oz/1⅓ cups buttermilk
whipped cream, chocolate leaves and fresh
    flowers, to decorate

FOR THE LEMON SYRUP
90 g/3½ oz/½ cup granulated sugar
120 ml/4 fl oz/½ cup water
30 ml/2 tbsp fresh lemon juice

FOR THE WHITE CHOCOLATE
    BUTTERCREAM (2 BATCHES)
2 x 350 g/12 oz white chocolate, chopped
2 x 500 g/1¼ lb/2½ cups cream cheese
2 x 275 g/10 oz unsalted butter,
    at room temperature
2 x 30 ml/2 tbsp fresh lemon juice
2 x 2.5 ml/½ tsp lemon essence

FOR ASSEMBLING
175 g/6 oz/⅔ cup lemon curd
50–115 g/2–4 oz/4–8 tbsp unsalted
    butter, softened

1 Mix the cakes in two batches. Preheat the oven to 180°C/350°F/ Gas 4. Grease and line a 30 cm/12 in cake tin.

2 Sift the flour, bicarbonate of soda and salt into a bowl. Heat the chocolate and cream over a medium heat, stirring, until smooth. Set aside to cool. Beat the butter with an electric mixer until creamy, add the sugar and beat for 2–3 minutes. Beat in the eggs. Slowly beat in the chocolate mixture, lemon essence and rind. On low speed, alternately beat in the flour in four batches and the buttermilk in three batches until smooth.

3 Pour into the tin and bake for 1 hour, until a metal skewer inserted into the centre comes out clean. Place the tin on a wire rack for 10 minutes, then turn out on to the rack to cool. Make a second cake. For the syrup, dissolve the sugar in the water over a medium heat, stirring. Off the heat, stir in the lemon juice and let cool.

4 To make the buttercream, put the chocolate in a bowl set over a pan of simmering water and stir until melted. Remove from the heat and cool slightly. Beat the cream cheese until smooth with an electric mixer. Gradually beat in the chocolate, then the butter, lemon juice and essence. Make a second batch.

5 To assemble, cut each cake in half horizontally. Spoon the syrup over each layer, allowing it to soak in, then repeat. Sandwich the layers of each cake together with lemon curd.

6 Gently beat the buttercream, then spread one-quarter on top of one cake. Place the other cake on top. Spread a little softened butter over the top and side. Chill for 15 minutes. Place the cake on a serving plate and spread the remaining buttercream on the top and side.

7 Spoon the whipped cream into a piping bag fitted with a small star nozzle and pipe shells carefully around the edges. Decorate with the leaves and flowers.

Chocolate Fruit Birthday Cake

A moist Madeira chocolate cake is decorated with eye-catching fruit moulded from coloured marzipan.

Serves 30

INGREDIENTS
1 quantity chocolate-flavoured
    Madeira Cake mix* (see Cook's Tip)
45 ml/3 tbsp Apricot Glaze*
1 quantity Marzipan*
1⅓ x quantity chocolate
    Fudge Frosting*
red, yellow, orange, green and purple
    food colouring
cloves
angelica strips
* See Basic Cakes, Icings & Glazes

1 Preheat the oven to 160°C/325°F/ Gas 3. Grease and line an 18 cm/7 in square cake tin. Spoon in the mixture, tap lightly to level the surface and bake for 1¼ hours, until a metal skewer inserted into the centre comes out clean. Place the tin on a wire rack for 10 minutes, then turn the cake out on to the rack to cool.

2 Cut a slice off the top of the cake to level, if necessary, then invert on to a 20 cm/8 in square cake board. Brush with the glaze. Roll out two-thirds of the marzipan on a surface lightly dusted with icing sugar to a 25 cm/ 10 in square. Use to cover and trim the cake. Reserve the trimmings.

3 Place the cake on a wire rack over a tray and pour over the warm fudge frosting, spreading quickly with a palette knife. Leave for 10 minutes, then return to the cake board.

4 Spoon the frosting from the tray into a piping bag fitted with a medium gâteau nozzle. Pipe a row of stars around the top edge and base of the cake. Leave to set.

5 Using the reserved marzipan, food colouring, cloves and angelica strips, model a selection of fruits.

6 Fit a strip of looped yellow ribbon around the cake and secure with a pin. Decorate the top of the cake with the colourful marzipan fruits.

COOK'S TIP: To flavour the Madeira Cake mix, omit the lemon rind and vanilla essence and stir in 15 ml/1 tbsp cocoa powder blended with 15 ml/1 tbsp boiling water just before adding the eggs.

First Published in 2000 by Hermes House
an imprint of
Anness Publishing Limited
Hermes House
88-89 Blackfriars Road
London SE1 8HA

A CIP catalogue record for this book is available from the British Library

Publisher: Joanna Lorenz
Editor: Valerie Ferguson
Series Designer: Bobbie Colgate Stone
Designer: Andrew Heath
Editorial Reader: Marion Wilson
Production Controller: Joanna King

Recipes contributed by: Sue Maggs, Sarah Maxwell,
Norma Miller, Janine Murfitt, Angela Nilsen, Louise Pickford,
Elizabeth Wolf-Cohen.

Photography: Edward Allwright, David Armstrong, Tim Hill,
Janine Hosegood, David Jordan.

1 3 5 7 9 10 8 6 4 2

Notes:
For all recipes, quantities are given in both metric and imperial measures and, where appropriate,
measures are also given in standard cups and spoons.
Follow one set, but not a mixture, because they are not interchangeable.

Standard spoon and cup measures are level.

1 tsp = 5 ml   1 tbsp = 15 ml

1 cup = 250 ml/8 fl oz

Australian standard tablespoons are 20 ml.
Australian readers should use 3 tsp in place of
1 tbsp for measuring small quantities of gelatine, cornflour, salt etc.

Medium eggs are used unless otherwise stated.